KIDS AROUND THE WORLD

KIDS IN EGYPT

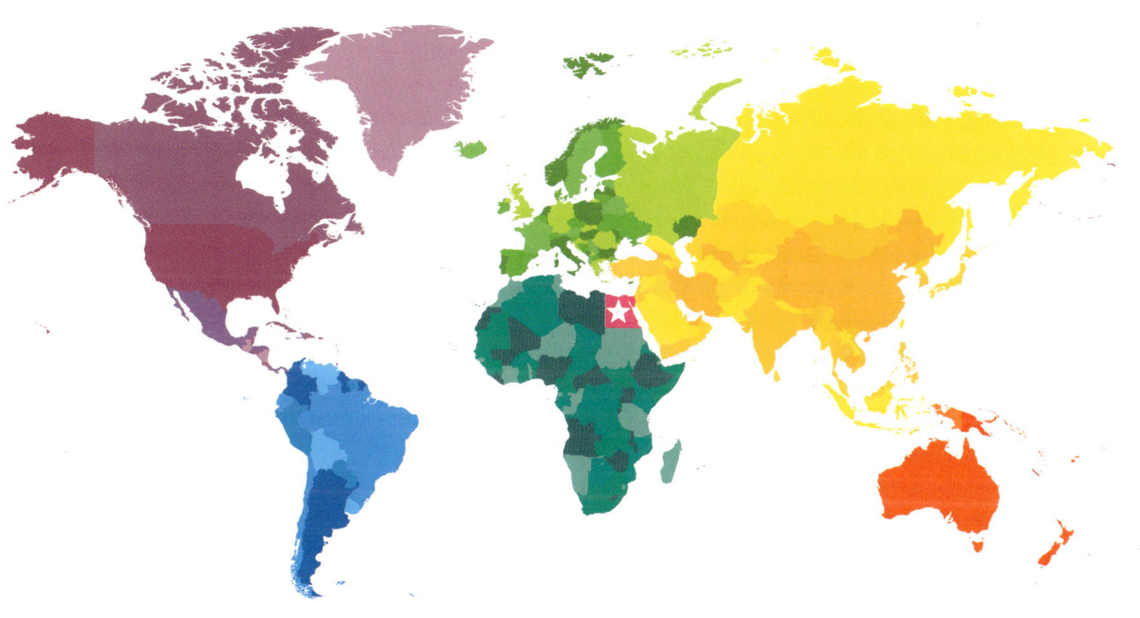

by Nikki Potts Ferguson

PEBBLE
a capstone imprint

Published by Pebble, an imprint of Capstone
1710 Roe Crest Drive, North Mankato, Minnesota 56003
capstonepub.com

Library of Congress Cataloging-in-Publication Data is available on the Library of Congress website.

ISBN: 9798875247897 (hardcover)
ISBN: 9798875247842 (paperback)
ISBN: 9798875247859 (ebook PDF)

Summary: Outstanding photographs and easy-to-understand text describe Egypt's landmarks, holidays, sports, foods, transportation, and more.

Editorial Credits
Editor: Erika L. Shores; Designer: Sarah Bennett; Media Researcher: Rebekah Hubstenberger; Production Specialist: Tori Abraham

Image Credits
Associated Press: Mohamed Elraai, 11; Getty Images: Ahmad Hasaballah, 28, Alex Pantling, 15, Craig Hastings, 6, David Sacks, cover (bottom), Fadel Dawod, 25, Hisham Ibrahim, 21, iStock/mit4711, 17, iStock/Mohammed Fouad, 24, iStock/temis, 14, iStock/Viktoriya Fivko, 18, KHALED DESOUKI/AFP, 27, Roger Anis, 26, Stuart Westmorland, 16; Newscom: Zhao Dingzhe/Xinhua News Agency, 12; Shutterstock: Alizada Studios, 13, bonchan, 19, Emily Marie Wilson, 9, Enez Selvi, 22, givaga, cover (top), Jojo Textures (rainbow border), cover and throughout, la.la.land, cover (globe icon), leshiy985, 20, Olga Vasilyeva, 10, paul prescott, 7, Pyty, back cover, 1, 4, Quisquilia, 5, RATOCA, 29, ViktoriyaFivko, 23

Capstone would like to thank Shaimaa El Banna for her assistance in creating this book.

Printed and bound in Malaysia. 006460

TABLE OF CONTENTS

Words in **bold** are in the glossary.

WELCOME TO EGYPT

Egypt is a country in northeastern Africa. It is known for the Nile River, museums, **ancient** pyramids, and more. Three pyramids make up the Pyramids of Giza.

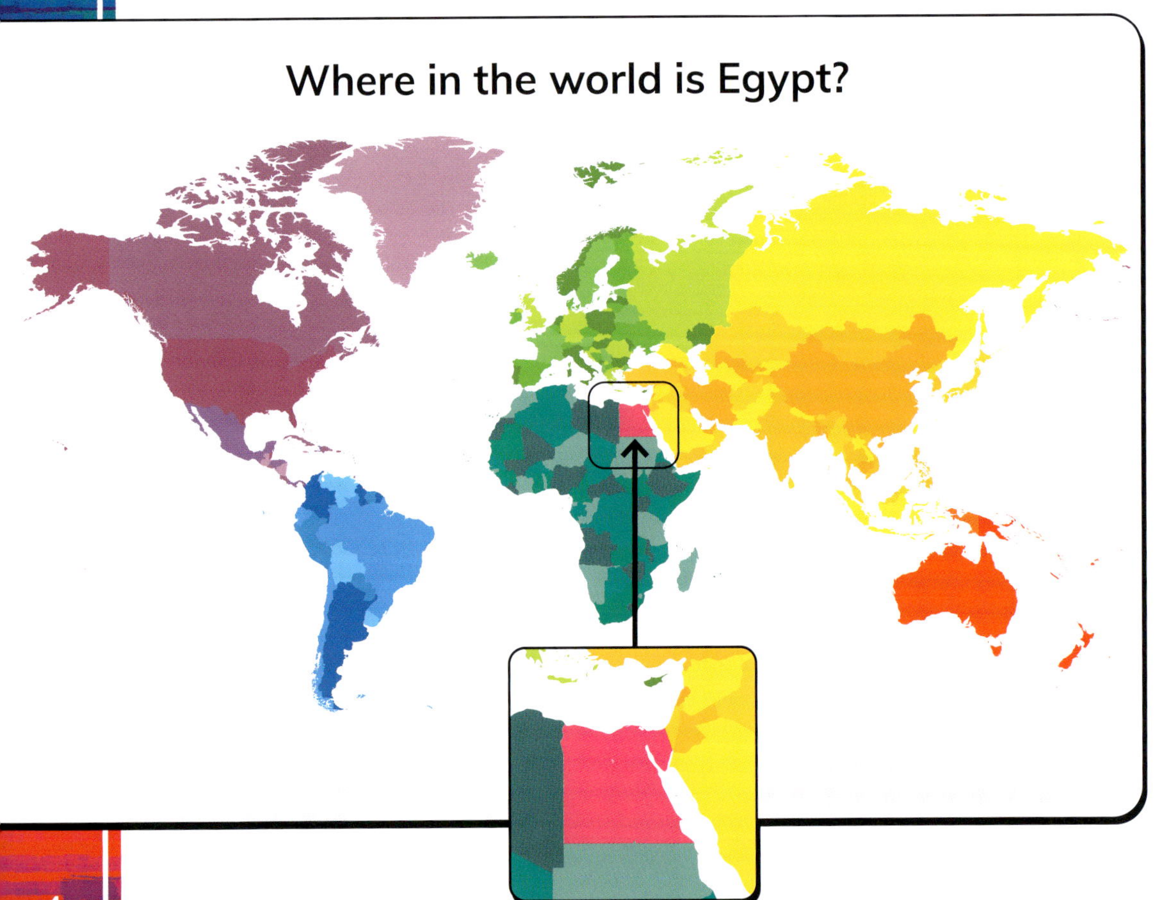

People have lived in Egypt for 400,000 years. Today, more than 111 million people live in Egypt. Let's learn what life is like for kids in Egypt.

AT HOME

Families in Egypt live in many different types of homes. Most people live in apartments in large cities. Some families live in houses. Most of the population is along the Nile River. It flows all the way from the country's southern border to the Mediterranean Sea in the north.

Kids usually live with their parents and siblings. They may also live with grandparents. Sometimes they live with or near aunts, uncles, and cousins too.

TRAVEL AND SCHOOL

Most kids take the bus to school in Egypt. A family member might also bring them. School is usually Saturday through Thursday. Friday is a day of rest. School days are six hours long.

Some kids go to public school. Others go to private school. At school, they learn math, social studies, science, and more. Kids also learn about their religion.

مدرسة حسني العقاد الخاصة
٤ش صدقي -السيدة زينب ت/٢٣٩٠٥٣٩٤
رياض أطفال -إبتدائي -إعدادى مشترك
ELAKKAD SCHOOLS @HOTMAIL.COM & WWW.HALAKKADSCHOOLS.COM

Kids in Egypt go to school for 12 years. They start school around age 4. At age 6, they start primary school. High school starts at age 15. It is also called secondary school. After high school, kids might go to a university. Others might learn a skill or trade.

Most Egyptian students wear uniforms. This might be a shirt with the school's logo on it. Students might wear flat, black shoes and pants or dresses.

FUN AND GAMES

Football is the most popular sport in Egypt. In the United States, football is called soccer. Kids in Egypt play football outdoors. Some schools have teams. Kids might play in leagues in the cities where they live.

Many people follow Egypt's national football team nicknamed the **Pharaohs**. The team has won the African Cup a record seven times.

Children play a board game outdoors.

Marble and board games are some favorite **pastimes**. Tennis, wrestling, and squash are also favorites.

Squash is played by two people on a court. They stand on the same side. One player hits a rubber ball with their racket. They hit the ball toward the wall in front of them. It bounces off and then it's the other player's turn to hit. Players score points. The person with the most wins the match.

Egyptian Museum

There are many famous landmarks in Egypt. Families might visit the Egyptian Museum in Cairo. Kids can learn about **tombs** and pharaohs. **Artifacts** from Egyptian pyramids tell us about how ancient Egyptians lived.

Colossi of Memnon

One of the oldest landmarks in Egypt is the Colossi of Memnon. Kids will see two statues of Pharaoh Amenhotep. One of the statues faces the Nile River. The other faces the sunrise.

FOOD IN EGYPT

Families in Egypt often eat beans and other vegetables at meals. Chickpeas are in many dishes. Koshari is made with chickpeas, pasta, onions, and rice. It has a vinegar, garlic, and tomato sauce on top.

koshari

Falafel is often served with pita bread.

Hummus is mashed chickpeas and spices. Falafel are deep-fried balls of beans mixed with herbs and spices.

Meat is also eaten at many meals in Egypt. Shawarma is seasoned meat. It is cooked on a **spit**. The meat is usually put on a bun or pita bread with sauce.

A man prepares shawarma meat.

Kebabs are made of pieces of meat and veggies. They are cooked on a stick called a skewer.

baklava

Sweets are popular in Egypt. Baklava is a sweet pastry. It has nuts and syrup in it. Omm Ali is a sweet bread pudding. It has sugar, nuts, and cream on top. Halawa is often eaten at breakfast. It is made of sesame seed paste and sugar.

Omm Ali

LET'S CELEBRATE

Ramadan is a **Muslim** holiday celebrated by kids and their families. Ramadan is the ninth month of the Islamic calendar. Muslims pray together in **mosques**. Adults and some kids **fast** during the day.

Eid al-Fitr is the end of Ramadan. Families celebrate for three days. They have large meals. Kids get new clothes and gifts. Kahk are special cookies made during this time. They might have dates or walnuts inside.

Sham el-Nessim is a national holiday celebrating the start of spring. It dates back to the time of the pharaohs. The holiday falls on the same day as Easter Monday. Kids and their families have an all-day picnic in the park. People eat and play games together.

Kids decorate eggs. They write wishes on them and hang them outside their house.

Christmas is a **Christian** holiday. In Egypt, many celebrate Christmas on January 7. Families gather for meals and go to church. Kids help their families decorate their homes with lights. They might put up a Christmas tree. Kids receive gifts and money on Christmas.

Egypt is an ancient country. It is a great place to live and visit. All ages enjoy the country's holidays, food, and landmarks. Pyramids, the Nile River, falafel, and more await in Egypt!

FAST FACTS

Location: Northeastern Africa

Capital: Cairo

Population: 111,247,248 people

Size: 386,662 square miles (1,001,450 square kilometers)

Official Language: Arabic

Currency: Egyptian pound

GLOSSARY

ancient (AYN-shunt)—from a long time ago

artifact (AR-tuh-fakt)—an object used in the past that was made by people

Christian (KRIS-chuhn)—a follower of the religion of Christianity

fast (FAST)—to give up eating for a period of time

mosque (MOSK)—a place of worship for Muslims

Muslim (MUHZ-luhm)—a follower of the religion of Islam

pastime (PASS-tym)—an activity that helps time pass in a good or happy way

pharaoh (FAIR-oh)—a king of ancient Egypt

spit (SPIT)—a long, pointed rod that holds meat for cooking

tomb (TOOM)—a room or building that holds a dead body and any items that were buried with that person

READ MORE

Golkar, Golriz. *Your Passport to Egypt*. North Mankato, MN: Capstone Press, 2022.

Gould, Sloane, and Kate Shoup. *Egypt*. New York: Cavendish Square, 2023.

Khalil, Aya. *Egypt*. Concord, MA: Barefoot Books, 2022.

INTERNET SITES

Egypt Facts
kids-world-travel-guide.com/egypt-facts.html

Kids Food Atlas
kidsfoodatlas.com/egypt

Understanding Ancient Egypt
historyforkids.net/ancient-egypt.html

INDEX

ABOUT THE AUTHOR

Nikki Potts Ferguson is a children's author and editor. Besides writing, she enjoys reading, crafting, and spending time with her family. Nikki lives in Kentucky with her husband, daughter, two cats, and dog.